MW00709697

Cuddling Is Like Chocolate

BY CHUCK GAIDICA
ILLUSTRATED BY JEFF COVIEO

FERNE PRESS

Cuddling Is Like Chocolate
Copyright © 2011 by Chuck Gaidica
Illustrated by Jeff Covieo
Layout and cover design by Kimberly Franzen
Illustrations created with digital graphics
Printed in the United States of America

Summary: An anecdotal look at how cuddling can make the world a better place.

Library of Congress Cataloging-in-Publication Data
Gaidica, Chuck
Cuddling Is Like Chocolate/Chuck Gaidica–First Edition
ISBN-13: 978-1-933916-78-1
1. Non-fiction. 2. Gift books. 3. Showing affection.
4. Cuddling.
I. Gaidica, Chuck II. Cuddling Is Like Chocolate
Library of Congress Control Number: 2010939919

FERNE PRESS

Ferne Press is an imprint of Nelson Publishing & Marketing
366 Welch Road, Northville, MI 48167
www.nelsonpublishingandmarketing.com
(248) 735-0418

First, I want to thank God for all He has done in my life, especially introducing me to my wife, Susan, who is my ultimate cuddle buddy! I dedicate this book to her.

I must acknowledge my family. My five children have always been an inspiration to me. As a dad, cuddling one of my children has always been a great reward. Whether reading a book to them or taking a nap, connected time with my kids has always been special. So, I celebrate my children, Riley, Kelsey, Matt, Charlie, and Tiffany, and Tiffany's husband, Adam.

I also must celebrate my brother and sister and their families. We were raised to hug and kiss, no matter what, and to this day that brings great joy.

My mom and dad, Chuck Sr. and Geri Gaidica, continue to cheer me on in all that I do. They never seem to mind hearing about my latest adventure in life. I love them dearly.

I want to thank illustrator Jeff Covieo, editor Kris Yankee, and publisher Marian Nelson. They are consummate professionals who were supportive and always willing to keep the ball rolling. I wish them every success in life.

Finally, I must acknowledge my late grandmother, Hilda Gaidica. While my mom and dad went off to work, Gram helped raise me and my siblings at various times. Cuddling was a way of life with her. Whether playing an old Bohemian game on my hand or cuddling with her in her favorite chair, I was privileged to share every moment with her. Even when she reached the twilight of her life and tried to explain to me that her illness would likely take her life, she held me and comforted me while I cried. She proved that cuddling those close to you is a lifelong mission that can bring comfort no matter the circumstances.

America's Cuddle Expert

"The temperature is dropping below thirty degrees tonight, and the winds will be picking up around midnight. It looks like it's a Cuddle Alert night. So cuddle up!" I announce at the weather map.

People have heard the words "Cuddle Alert" for over twenty years. While sitting at my Little Rock, Arkansas, weather forecast office in the early 1980s, I decided to create a fun way to describe cold weather. I'd grown up in Chicago, where winters were bold and often brutal. In Little Rock, winters were often cold and drab; a little freezing rain here, a small amount of snow there, but rarely a dramatic winter event.

One day it hit me: Create a fun phrase that could be used when it gets cold. "Cuddle Alert" was born. I issued Cuddle Alerts when the temperature dipped below average. This also meant that I could issue a Cuddle Alert during any season, as long as the temperature dipped below average. So, a chilly night in the middle of summer could qualify. As a matter of fact, I kid people who I meet that I have the power to issue a Cuddle Alert any time I feel like it. That gets a big smile and often a look of anticipation! By definition, the "alert" gives permission to cuddle with someone or something. This covered all of the bases. You could cuddle a person, your dog, or even a stuffed animal. You could grab a teddy bear and cuddle all night through the cold. Lo and behold, it was a hit! I have continued to issue Cuddle Alerts throughout

1

my television career, even on the weekend *Today Show*.

But what exactly is cuddling?

Cuddling is different than hugging or a quick squeeze. It isn't even a hug, but it can include a hug. *Webster's Ninth New Collegiate Dictionary* defines cuddle as "to hold close for warmth or comfort or in affection: to lie close or snug: nestle or snuggle."

When I refer to cuddling, I see it as a long and tender hug. Or, it can be simply a shared moment. The act of cuddling implies taking some amount of time to connect or reconnect with someone. The key to this is time: taking the time to connect with someone.

The act of cuddling implies taking some time to sit or lie down with somebody, get in a comfortable and cozy position, and snuggle in for a bit.

In my case, I need to be cuddled. The funny thing is that I don't require hugging from strangers. Hugging others is not a turnoff; it's just not my thing. But I love to cuddle with my wife, my kids, and my dogs. Last year, my wife and I set out to find new furniture for our family room. We often watch TV in this room and love to play and relax here, too. To our surprise, the furniture that we chose for our family room is designed for cuddling. My wife and I exchanged looks of disbelief when the salesperson told us that our furniture was called a "cuddler sofa." This particular type of sectional sofa has a piece on the end that allows for two adults (or several kids) to cuddle and watch a movie or favorite show.

It was our destiny to own furniture with the word "cuddle" in the name. We use the furniture frequently and always try to cuddle. When cuddling with my wife, under a warm blanket on that micro-fiber sofa, it is hard to finish a movie. At my age and with my busy days, it is hard not to move from cuddling to snoring. Either way, the furniture was worth the money!

Most people like to be held close for comfort and warmth. As we grow from babies, some of us get lots of hugs, kisses, and cuddles. As we enter puberty, it sometimes becomes awkward to cuddle with Mom or Dad for various reasons. When we marry or find a great partner, we are ready and often aching for cuddling, and it may not come as often as we like as the years fly by.

With all of life's busyness—work, kids, errands, cell phones, email, preparing meals, working out or around the house—when do we find time to just sit and catch our breath? When do we find the time to cuddle with somebody, cuddle with anybody? Make time to cuddle. Build it into your day. This strong connection will help you feel loved and wanted. Cuddling with somebody gives him or her a boost, too.

If you get to cuddle frequently in your relationship, tell your partner how much you like it and appreciate it. As we grow older, we may lose our best cuddle buddy. But, that doesn't mean cuddling has to end. At every stage in life, we need to have a place for cuddling.

As I mentioned, cuddling can be done with somebody, especially your spouse. Since cuddling doesn't necessarily lead to sexy time, you can cuddle with anyone, like your grandma, or even a pet, teddy bear, or pillow. To avoid having to cuddle with just a pillow, this book is written to inspire all of us to find somebody important to cuddle with now.

I have to admit that I am one of the "cuddle needy" among us. I require human touch. Beyond that, I require a loving and caring nuzzle. I know, I sound like your pet dog or horse. A nuzzle implies using my nose to push and burrow into a spot that grows comfortable while cuddling. I don't care which part of my body or your body initiates the cuddling process, just start it. It's like a dance. Find the right position, hold on to the other person just the right way, and find that unique combination of holding on that feels so perfect. Cuddling is very much the same. I start to work at it and I just know when it feels right. It makes my soul feel better. It makes me feel connected to the one person in the world that matters most above all others.

Sometimes cuddling doesn't just happen. Sometimes you do need to tell your spouse or significant other that you need to cuddle.

I became interested in the concept of cuddling over time. Little did I know many years ago that a fun little phrase that I created would pertain to me because I love to cuddle.

This book is going to explore cuddling. I'll talk about why it is important to us and why our spouses or loved ones need to know more about cuddling. I'll show you why cuddling can make a child's day and what the research shows on this topic.

"Hugs can do great amounts of good, especially for children."
~Princess Diana

You will read about babies who are cuddled from birth at orphanages as opposed to those who are left alone. They grow up more loved and become more loving. Research shows that seniors who sit with, hug, or cuddle with a relative, or even a visiting dog from a shelter, report feeling better. What happens inside us? Why is cuddling so important?

After you read this book, I hope you can use the information to your advantage. I hope that you share the book with your spouse, a loved one, or a friend. You will be ready to discover a lifetime of Cuddle Alerts!

THE DISCONNECT OF "FUTURE SHOCK"

In a world where we have more opportunities to communicate through social networks, are we in a state of information overload? Do we need to catch our breath? Do we need to stop calling and texting our children or brothers and sisters while they play in the same house we are in? Technology is a great thing. It can make us more productive and efficient. But technology like cell and smart phones, along with social networking websites, are distracting us from being face to face with one another. When was the last time you made a point to sit down next to someone, hold them, cuddle them, look them in the eyes, and hold their hands? How safe and connected you both would feel in this world of uncharted change.

Do you ever ask somebody how his or her day is going? Or ask them how they feel? Do you really care? If most of us answered that question honestly, the answer wouldn't be the one we are looking for after all. Most of us just want to act polite and move on.

But it goes deeper than that. We are becoming less involved with people we are intimately involved with on a daily basis. Our kids tune out and walk right past us on the way to their rooms to electronically communicate with God knows how many people in just minutes. Our spouses may seem constantly preoccupied while we try to talk to them or invite them to watch a movie with us. These are not new issues. But today's busy lifestyles and high-tech gadgets have complicated matters.

Back in 1970, Alvin Toffler wrote a book entitled *Future Shock*. One of the points Toffler argued was that we were becoming less involved with each other. Remember, this book was written in 1970. Many people still lived in neighborhoods with sidewalks. Grandma and Grandpa may have lived upstairs or down the street.

But Toffler saw this phenomenon coming like a freight train. He worried and wrote that people were becoming increasingly disconnected. He suggested that our relationships with each other were more and more "fragmented and modular." It's important to remember that he was thinking about and researching this book in the 1960s. If somebody wrote this book today or talked about this idea with you at a party, wouldn't you think the concepts were developed for today's world?

He writes, "we are not sufficiently involved with our fellow man."

Toffler offered his own opinions and cited many psychologists. He argued that the increasing transience of our relationships was leading to the temporary feeling many people had about relationships. He supported the notion that transience actually leads to contact with more people. But this exposure to huge numbers of people leads us to seek less contact with them, not more.

Does every generation feel this way? What if we lived in 1900? What kind of rapid change could our minds handle?

In 1903, the Wright Brothers took their first "flying machine" for a successful ride in the sky. People started flying on airplanes. And within sixty-one years, a man had landed on the moon.

In 1908, Henry Ford delivered his first Model T for $825. Within four years, the price had dropped to $575 and sales skyrocketed. Thousands of people were now driving cars.

Were people in the early 1900s feeling a future shock as they watched the start of a new century and industrial revolutions change the world?

So, now we fast-forward to today. Toffler's words are eerily prescient.

Do we feel the same way as our cell phones with video come to life, our newspapers and magazines disappear, and the stock market tanks right in front of our eyes?

Toffler also reflected on a throwaway society. It may have been a building trend and even a concern, but how could he know people today would be consuming and buying products for a few hundred bucks and literally throwing them away in a couple of years?

To say that Toffler was ahead of his time is a gross understatement. He saw the combined effects of transience, a throwaway mentality, and information overload leading to a future shock. His warnings were clear. An age was coming where change would happen so quickly that our minds just couldn't keep up.

Aren't we there?

If progress is to occur, aren't products and services supposed to improve at a steady pace?

Electronic mail has led to Twitter and social networking. But our minds can only progress so fast. Are we in the game or just sitting by in shock? Are we in a state of information overload? Do we need to catch our breath?

I think that we are overloaded, almost every day it seems.

This is future shock. And catching our breath only comes when we go to sleep at night.

Toffler argued that society was undergoing a rapid change in structure and relationship. Future shock!

He pointed out the fast rate of both societal and technological change and how it was leaving people feeling broken and disoriented, completely stressed out. Future shock!

One thing is certain: change. As the world continues to change, we can't just hang on to our electronic toys or money; we must hold on to each other, maybe for dear life!

There is an antidote to future shock: We need to cuddle again. We need to take time to sit with our kids and hold them tight and let them tell us about their troubles and triumphs. We need to sit with our spouse, nuzzle close, and watch that movie or sporting event. We need to draw strength from each other's calm.

Life changes at the speed of light. Our relationships change—suffer, some would argue—in the process. I have seen kids in the same room text each other—they didn't speak to each other but used their cell phones instead. Parents don't call out to kids to come to dinner; they text them.

Technology disconnects us on one hand and reconnects us on the other. Toffler didn't argue for the status quo, however. He suggested that we embrace change. I would suggest we embrace each other!

Computers and cell phones may all have a hand in creating distance between us.

But look at what they have helped us achieve: social networking, finding old friends, keeping in touch with our kids after school. So, the world isn't all bad. But if we are not careful, sitting next to each other, holding hands, and cuddling while watching a movie will become a faint memory that only pops up when we hear our favorite love song on the radio.

We need to cuddle again.

Is It the Right Time?

We know that there is a time and place for offering affection or even a simple touch.

While many societal issues interfere with our own human intimacy, there are some cultures that hug and kiss a lot—including the men. Some of that behavior has been carried into America. But for any number of reasons, some of us are afraid to touch. We put up a wall. Our own innate sense of right and wrong may be clouded by our own judgments or what we hear in the media. We question ourselves, "What will others think of us?"

Here are a few common fears:

- If you hug a member of the same sex, you might be gay.
- If you touch a little boy or girl and offer affection, you might be a pedophile. We are shown internet predators weekly on television.
- If you touch a child, you might be accused of child abuse.

We don't know whom to touch and when it is okay. More likely, most of us know the rules and just avoid the entire issue. We should do more to encourage hugging, cuddling, and showing affection appropriately. We don't seem to be afraid at weddings or funerals. Why are we so afraid otherwise?

Children don't have the same issues. Jesus called little children to Him and hugged them. He told his disciples that unless they changed and became like little children, they couldn't enter the kingdom of heaven. He wanted them to have childlike trust and faith. He wanted them to have childlike love!

As good role models, it is our responsibility to show appropriate affection to our children. Cuddling with our loved ones will teach them as well as help them to feel wanted and comforted. If someone we love is hurting, we hold them, rub their back, and tell them it will be okay. The same is true when we aren't hurting but just need that comforting, loving closeness.

As you will see in the next few pages, there are proven, scientific reasons to cuddle. After you understand a few of them, you may be reading the rest of this book in someone's lap.

Why Cuddle?

Cuddling offers affection and warmth. Even if you are going back over last night's cuddle in your mind, it will feel good again.

Cuddly

"I am from Michigan and my wife is from Lithuania, so we know what cold winters are like! Because Michigan winters seem to last forever, cuddling isn't just fun, it's necessary for survival. Ever since we can remember, we have used the name 'cuddly' to ensure that we don't forget to stay close and avoid freezing.

"Even the Bible encourages us to cuddle. Ecclesiastes 4:11 says, 'And on a cold night, two under the same blanket can gain warmth from each other. But how can one be warm alone?' So there you have it, Cuddliness is next to Godliness!"

~Jimi and Vaiva Varner, Livonia, Michigan

What Is So Good about Cuddling?

- Cuddles are free to give and free to get.
- A cuddle can make you feel like a million bucks.
- There is no such thing as a bad cuddle.
- Cuddles are green; they are completely renewable and energy efficient.
- There is no time limit on cuddling.

- Cuddling can comfort.
- You can cuddle almost anything.
- Cuddling can keep you warm and warm things up.
- You can watch a movie and cuddle.
- There is no minimum or maximum age requirement.
- Cuddling is best when the weather takes a turn.
- Cuddling is naturally sweet and fat free.

Cuddling Is Good for You, Medically Speaking

Studying the "Cuddle Hormone" at a Touch Institute?

C uddling is more than skin deep. But the cuddle process has to start somewhere. According to a recent segment on the National Public Radio program *Morning Edition* with Michelle Trudeau (September 20, 2010), we have to understand the process of touch before we can understand why we feel so good after a coach's high-five or a loving caress.

NPR talked to Tiffany Field, the director of the Touch Research Institute in Miami, Florida. She points out that understanding touch starts with the understanding of skin. As Field notes, the skin is our largest organ, covering about twenty square feet.

Field says that when somebody touches us, that point of contact on your skin, the pressure point of inception, causes pressure receptors to be stimulated. The receptors send a signal directly to the brain, heart, and other organs.

One particular part of the brain that receives the signal is called the vagus nerve. This nerve, or bundle of nerves really, can send other signals to slow the heart and even decrease blood pressure.

Field points out that experiments have shown that when a person is given stressful tasks like public speaking, being hugged by or holding hands with a partner just before the stressful act lowered blood pressure and heart rate, suggesting lowered stress. According to DePauw University psychologist Matt Hertenstein, handholding or hugging reduces the secretion of the stress hormone cortisol. In addition, Hertenstein told NPR that friendly touch can also increase the release of oxytocin, also known as the "cuddle hormone."

Now that's what I am talking about, a cuddle hormone!

Oxytocin can promote various feelings of trust, devotion, and bonding, according to Hertenstein. He says the cuddle hormone makes us feel closer to one another.

- Cuddling is healthy for the mind and heart.
- Cuddling can reduce stress.
- Cuddling can relieve depression and the feeling of being disconnected.
- Cuddling can help boost your immune system.
- Cuddling can even help induce sleep.

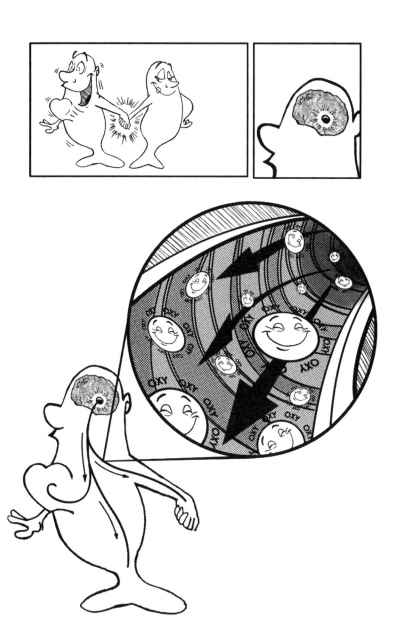

Cuddle Fast Fact:
The Cuddle Hormone Oxytocin

The hypothalamus gland in the brain naturally produces oxytocin. This hormone is released in women in a variety of situations, such as childbirth and sex. According to researchers, men and women benefit from oxytocin and its male counterpart, vasopressin.

The brain can affect behavior, and behavior can also affect the brain. Changing your behavior by including more cuddling can produce these hormones and help inspire increased feelings of fondness and tenderness. As love, admiration, and affection grow, more oxytocin is released and even more affection can follow. The cuddle hormone is powerful, so snuggle up!

"At the touch of love, everyone becomes a poet."

~Plato

Medical Support

Many claims have been made about the medical benefits of cuddling. Some say cuddling is a miracle medicine that can relieve many emotional and physical problems. It has been said that cuddling could make you live longer, cure depression, increase your sex life, protect your body against illness, and even help you sleep.

According to researchers at the University Medical Center of Southern Nevada, when a person is touched, the amount of hemoglobin in the blood shows a dramatic increase. Oxygen is carried by hemoglobin to all organs of the body. The heart and brain are obviously influenced. This rapid increase in oxygen can help prevent diseases and speed up recovery.

Cuddle Fast Fact

Nurses associations have endorsed therapeutic touch in patients after learning about the way it can increase oxygen flow through the human body.

Cuddle Fast Fact

Researchers at the University of North Carolina–Chapel Hill looked at two groups of adults with spouses or long-term partners. One group was told to hold hands with their partners while watching a pleasant video and to hug for twenty seconds afterward. The other group rested quietly without their partners.

The people who rested alone had blood pressure rates that were double those of the huggers. Their heart rates also increased more.

Doctors say it is more evidence that people are hardwired to be social animals. We really do feel better while touching. It can help your heart!

Cuddlers Needed

Each year for about the past fifteen years, I have had the honor of presenting awards to health care volunteers. Each volunteer has thousands of hours of service. Some work in the gift shop, some create new programs, and some serve at the greeting desk. The recognition luncheon that honors these great folks is called "Thanks for Giving." One new effort recently developed for volunteers allows for cuddling on the pediatric floor.

"Cuddlers" are recruited as unique caregivers who are allowed to offer comfort throughout various floors, including pediatric transplant, cardiac, and intensive care units. Some hospitals have seen such success with this program that they have allowed the cuddlers access to the entire hospital.

The Cuddler

Grandma Huggs

Bella

Some of the cuddlers are amazed at how infrequently some of the parents visit their own children. This volunteer cuddle brigade not only provides a warm touch but also learns about each child's fears and dreams.

No matter what the age or health of a patient, the cuddlers prove to be essential in the health care process. With the increase of cuddlers in the hospitals, it is clear that hospital administrators are convinced more than ever that cuddling promotes healing!

Cuddling and Your Relationships

To all the men out there, let me clue you in on something: most women, especially those in long-term relationships, want to cuddle and hug. It doesn't have to be sensual or sexual. Cuddling indicates to your partner, "I love you, and I want to spend some time with you."

Adding intimacy to your relationship, like cuddling, hugging, and kissing, will help make your partner feel closer and more connected to you.

If you spontaneously add a peck on her cheek or actually take a moment to sit down next to your wife and cuddle, you score points and reduce stress. Less stress equals a better chance at sexy time!

According to polls from various sources, cuddling routinely outranks candlelight dinners and sending flowers. Cuddling scores higher than trips away and long walks together.

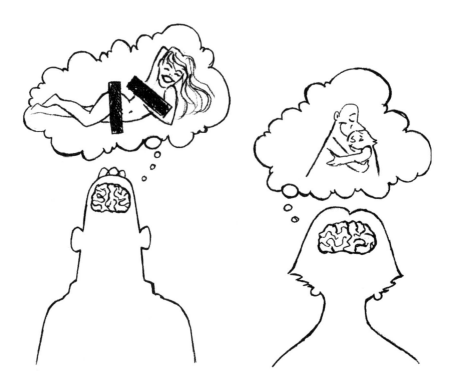

In almost every poll, cuddling outscores sex. In one poll, cuddling outscored even this response: "hot, passionate sex." How can this be? The research shows that what women really want is cuddling and a movie.

All About the Girl

"Women sometimes act out, and men get frustrated. They don't get that all we want is a few seconds, for you to be all about the girl—to snuggle her and give her kisses."

~Katharine McPhee, singer and famed
American Idol contestant, *Stuff Magazine*

Cuddle Fast Fact: A Women's Study for Men

A 2006 study by the Berman Center for Women's Health in Chicago can help all men. The study showed that couples that routinely indulge in spur-of-the-moment, non-sexual physical affection are more satisfied with their relationships. If you don't understand cuddling, you should see how it leads to a happy girlfriend. Guys, if your girlfriend is happy, the relationship is happy, and you, my friend, are happy. It's time to cuddle.

Sex, Bowling, and Cuddles

Several years ago, in 1985 to be exact, two columnists asked their readers what they thought about cuddling. Ann Landers, one of the most successful advice columnists ever, along with her sister Abigail Van Buren (of "Dear Abby" fame) wrote a column asking their readers the following: Would you be content to be held close and treated tenderly and forget about "the act" (i.e., sexy time)?

Over ninety thousand women responded, and 72 percent answered yes, including twenty-six thousand under the age of forty.

Women have been saying for years, and still say, that they would rather cuddle with their partner than have sex! And this poll or survey is no slouch. A sample of ninety thousand women is huge. Most nationwide polls for products or political candidates have a much smaller sample, usually under one thousand people.

One woman wrote a note with her response to the Landers survey:

"I hate sex. I was relieved when my husband died. My present husband is on heart pills and impotent. It's heaven to be held and cuddled."

Now this is a bit dramatic, but men need to understand their women.

Landers received sixty-eight thousand responses from men, too. Only 8 percent answered yes to the cuddle question, and most of those men were over sixty years old.

One man wrote, "The older I get, the longer it takes. But I won't settle for cuddling until it's all I can do."

Another man wrote this:

"My wife claims that holding her close is nothing more than 'upper persuasion for lower invasion.'"

Now for the beer, bowling, and sex part of the story (I added the beer myself).

In another column that followed the Ann Landers column, nationally syndicated writer Mike Royko asked his male audience to reply to this question: "Do you prefer sex with your mate or some other kind of recreational activity?"

Over ten thousand men responded, with 66 percent preferring sex. Bowling, drinking, golf, cuddling, or just about any other activity tallied just 22 percent. Those who couldn't make up their minds or preferred "other" came in at 12 percent.

We have confirmation that men are indeed from Mars and women are just right. If all women want to do is cuddle once in a while, what is the big deal? Does this idea detract from our masculinity? Are we afraid that our wives will tell their girlfriends that we cuddle?

In Royko's column, he cites a reader named Sherman of Glen Ellyn, Illinois, who writes, "After thirty-five years of marriage, I have come to the conclusion that there are no frigid wives, but only inconsiderate, ignorant, and boorish husbands who neither know nor care about the sexual needs, responses, or desires of their wives. Get with it, gentlemen!"

So, there is a call to action for all guys everywhere: it is time to cuddle!

"I think men are often sex experts, but intimacy apprentices. Men may have had lots of sex, know how special it can be, but are still learning the ABCs when it comes to connecting emotionally."

~John H. Driggs, clinical social worker and human sexuality expert

CUDDLING AND CHILDREN

Better Children

"Cuddling and caressing make the growing child feel secure and is an aid in self-esteem."
~Dr. Achal Bhagat, psychiatrist, www.lifepositive.com

Cuddle Your Kids

I have five kids and have always enjoyed holding them and cuddling. It makes me feel better and likely makes them feel better too. It may not surprise you that scientists and doctors have documented the benefits of cuddling our children. These social benefits can last for many years afterward. A link has been shown between love and attention in children's early years and their emotional responses later in life.

Scientists at the University of Wisconsin–Madison took eighteen children all around four and a half years old. All were born in orphan-

29

ages and had missed out on the physical contact provided by a mom and dad. All had since been adopted and given lots of love and attention. As the children aged, some displayed unusual behavior, such as seeking comfort from perfect strangers.

Now, here is where it gets interesting. As compared to a group of children from "normal" backgrounds, the orphaned children were found to have significantly lower levels of a certain hormone that is deemed critical in recognizing people in a social environment.

All of the children—the orphaned children and the children brought up by their own parents—were then tested together. They were all placed on the laps of their mother or a female stranger for a half hour. They played games and received physical contact with the women. This included touching, patting, tickling, and whispering. Hormone levels were measured again. Oxytocin levels rose, as expected, in the kids brought up from birth by their families. The orphanage kids saw no similar result.

According to the researchers, these findings may help explain why children who are neglected may have a harder time forming secure relationships when they get older.

Can we now imagine the gigantic problem we may be facing in cities all across America? Not only in orphanages but in households across the land. We now have clear signals that kids who are neglected and are not touched and loved may grow up ill equipped to touch and love their own children. It is a vicious cycle that may explain much as we watch babies having babies. We need to encourage cuddling of our children.

"A baby is born with a need to be loved, and never outgrows it."
~Frank A. Clark, author of the
Country Parson cartoon

A Mother's Touch

A mother's touch during childhood can go a long way. New research tells us that when a mother comforts her child after injuries, like kissing a boo-boo, it can have a lasting effect by boosting immunities that help fight disease. The study found that adults who said they had a warm bond with their mom had fewer markers for inflammation.

Good Health Segment
Local 4 News, WDIV-TV-Detroit

Our Destiny Is to Live and Love

I recently read an article about what I consider to be a miracle. The author, Professor Donald DeMarco, wrote about twin baby girls who can teach us so much about life.

Kyrie and Brielle Jackson were born three months premature. At birth, Kyrie weighed just over two pounds. Brielle was even lighter than her sister and had additional health problems. Both were placed in separate incubators in order to survive. Within a month, Brielle became even more fragile and was critical. Her parents watched in fear.

While Kyrie grew stronger, Brielle grew weaker. A nurse at the hospital suggested a very unorthodox method of treatment. She asked the parents if the twins could be placed in the same incubator. The parents said yes.

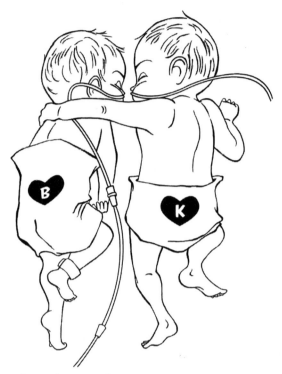

As soon as the girls were close to each other, Brielle, the weaker of the two, cuddled up to Kyrie and her vital signs improved. As time went on, the girls' health improved and they were released from the hospital. After they got home, the girls' parents placed them in the same bed and they continued to cuddle their way back to health. According to their parents, even after five years, the girls were sleeping together and cuddling.

Over the course of time, the hospital where the girls were born continued to place siblings side by side for improved health. The hospital program expanded to include other twins, triplets, and even quadruplets. The hospital learned what the Jackson family had learned: there are natural benefits to cuddling.

Further research by nurse Mary Whalen confirmed other benefits that premature twins enjoyed when cuddling in the same bed. The twins' vital signs improved greatly. They took to feeding better. They appeared less agitated and were more likely to have a shorter hospital stay.

A miracle? You be the judge. But DeMarco cites more research that pertains to us, too. He points out that science shows that hugging in various ways strengthens us. Our immune systems improve, we sleep better, and we are less stressed.

Two premature baby girls knew instinctively what we sometimes ignore. Kyrie and Brielle knew the power of cuddling and how it would make them better. We are stronger when we are connected. The Bible teaches us that a rope woven of multiple strands is not broken quickly. We are stronger together. The twins proved it. We just need to apply what we have learned to others in our families.

Cuddling works!

Give Me a Hug

"We need four hugs a day for survival. We need eight hugs a day for maintenance. We need twelve hugs a day for growth."

~Virginia Satir, family therapist,
www.lifepositive.com

ANIMALS AND THEIR LOVING CUDDLES

I recently talked to a college friend of mine, Myra. Like many families, hers has been affected by cancer. Myra and her highly trained therapy dog, Frisco, reach out to cancer patients in the Grand Rapids, Michigan, area. Myra is astounded by the healing power of her dog.

Frisco, a golden retriever, is no small dog. But Myra explains that on her command, this special dog has been allowed on patients' beds and to cuddle next to the patients. Frisco even knows how to crawl under tubes and intravenous lines to get close for cuddle therapy. How important is this therapy? Read the following stories, which Myra wrote about three of Frisco's patient encounters.

Praying for an Angel

One day, while we were walking the halls of a cancer center, a young woman was kneeling outside a room. Frisco crawled over and put his head in her lap. I was embarrassed, because he wasn't through with training.

People are supposed to come to

him, not the other way around. But, before I could pull him away, the young woman held her hand up and asked me to stop. She looked at me with tears in her eyes and said, "My father is dying of cancer, and I was praying for an angel. God sent me one with four legs and fur." She wrapped her arms around Frisco, and we sat quietly.

Facing Fears

Another time while walking the hospital hallways, a woman was being wheeled into surgery. She saw Frisco and grabbed my arm in passing. "I would like to hug your dog." Frisco obliged and put his head near her own. I don't think there was a dry eye nearby, including my own! She looked at everybody and said, "Now I am ready to face the surgery."

Frisco Doesn't Care

Frisco and I walked through an infusion room one day and met a beautiful young woman. She waved us over and grabbed Frisco for a hug. Frisco licked her face and then her bald head.

She turned to her mother and said, "See, Frisco doesn't care whether I have hair or not."

Frisco doesn't care about how much money you make or what your physical condition is; he just loves and gives hugs. And for the people he meets, it makes all the difference—one wag at a time!

If We Could Talk to the Animals

Other important research shows that just displaying animals in doctor's offices and waiting rooms calms people down.

A University of Minnesota study showed that just having gerbils, finches, or fish on display was enough to bring down the stress levels of waiting patients.

We often take for granted the connection we make with our own dogs and cats. Just walking, grooming, or petting them is enough for both of us to feel good. Our pets can make us feel safe, too. The idea that they are guarding the house says much. Their unconditional love is legend. Our pets offer us a way to feel wanted and provide us with an extra bond that even our own spouses can't explain. What better therapy for you and your pet than to cuddle?

If you have had a bad day or feel lonely, you can get a boost! Is there anything better than cuddling with your dog on the floor, especially on a cold winter day when the sun has heated the floor around you?

In 1990, researchers studied one thousand Medicare patients. They found that dog owners visited their doctors 16 percent less than those who did not own dogs. These researchers published their findings in the *Journal of Personality and Social Psychology*. The study suggested that the pets reduced stress from major illness, divorce, and family tragedies like death. It further suggested that we humans would be better equipped to deal with all of the above if we had our dogs to turn to—or cuddle with!

Cuddling Runs a Fowl

ENOUGH WITH THE
DIRT ALREADY!!!

If you're a chicken, you can get dirty cuddling. No, not that kind of dirty; I mean the chickens can get covered in dirt. On a hot, still afternoon, the chickens dig a hole under the ferns at the edge of the woods. They lie down next to each other to enjoy the shade and cool breezes that come their way. They dig in and start to cuddle. The chickens don't stay still forever, as they tend to adjust and scoot closer to each other. They roll from side to side until they get even more comfortable, kicking dirt up and out from underneath themselves. They have one goal in mind: dig down deeper and find cooler ground.

At first, you would think that a hen lying there, getting covered in flying dirt, would mind the entire process. She doesn't seem to mind. After a few minutes of relaxing, she returns the favor of cuddling ever more closely with the other chickens. This is a good afternoon for a chicken.

~Chris Gaidica, web developer and gentleman farmer,
Tustin, Michigan

New Ways to Incorporate Cuddling into Our Lives

Trends come and go. One recent new trend is the cuddle party. In a city near you, watch for a room full of pajama-wearing folks who want to cuddle with strangers. If you don't have a cuddle buddy at home, why not throw a party? Self-described relationship coaches invented cuddle parties. I am not sure how you become that kind of coach.

These parties begin with a "welcome circle" that is led by a facilitator. Safe space is provided around participants as they introduce each other. An icebreaker and a few fun games follow this, and the cuddle party rules are explained.

Then for two hours, you can socialize and cuddle to your heart's content. But, the facilitators (or referees as I like to think of them) keep participants on track. At the end, a "closing circle" is formed to recap the evening.

Rules of a cuddle party:
- You don't have to cuddle anybody.
- Make sure your hygiene is acceptable (no body odor).
- You must ask permission to touch somebody and get a firm "yes."
- PJs stay on the whole time.
- Laughter and tears are okay.
- Massages and foot rubs are just fine.
- Holding hands is good.
- Cuddle away!

For more information about cuddle parties, please see www.cuddleparty.com.

A Whole Day for Hugging

How about an entire day made for hugging?

Watch for National Hugging Day on January 21. You can celebrate in many different countries, too. Many nursing homes, churches, and groups follow this relatively new holiday (established in 1986). Participants can't wait to hug somebody, anybody. Extending this idea to a cuddle with your senior mom or dad is a pleasant thought. Cuddling your spouse and child is good, too, and the action of cuddling gives back.

Yes, that will do nicely! Reminds me very much of my Edna's bottom.

Missing You

A new feature of travel in the UK Travelodge hotel chain is a specially designed cuddle pillow called the "cuddillow." This is not a joke! Research showed that more than half of all hotel respondents felt lonely sleeping without their partner. Sixty-three percent said that they *needed* a bedtime cuddle. Many said that they spray their partner's cologne or perfume on the cuddillow to help them fall asleep.

Many people polled said that they actually fantasized about "who" their cuddillow was supposed to be. For women, Johnny Depp and George Clooney came to mind. For male cuddlers, Angelina Jolie topped the list.

How to Give a Cuddle

Here are a few tips:

- Never force a cuddle. If your partner is uncomfortable, not in the mood, or pulls away, they are not ready to cuddle.

- If your arm, pillow, sheets, or something else is in the way of a cuddle, fix it. Comfort is key to a good cuddle.

- Don't fake your feelings. Whether giving or receiving a cuddle, you can't have a wall put up. Your partner will be able to tell if you don't feel affectionate toward them.

- Be tender and soft. You must relax and pull the other person toward you. Whether sitting on the sofa watching a movie or spooning in bed, get into the moment.

- Cuddling should not be fast. Make the time to relax and cuddle with that special person. If you sit for a minute and run off to the next thing, you not only ruin the cuddle, but you create anxiety and maybe even resentment.

- Look for opportunities to cuddle for a long time. Romantic movies are a great chance. You will have a couple of hours, a blanket can be used if it's cold, and you can relax and enjoy the movie.

It's Time to Cuddle Again

Now that you know why you should cuddle, what are you waiting for?

Even though chocolate produces the same effect as cuddling, wouldn't it be better to wrap your arms around someone (or something) that you love and give a squeeze?

It doesn't really matter if you are a man or a woman; cuddling is healthy and will likely lead to a stronger bond with your spouse, kids, or other family members.

Some will think that there is little time to invest in such an idea. But just like saving for your retirement, cuddling frequently builds up the points that help create a secure and long-lasting relationship.

Don't be afraid to ask for a cuddle, and certainly don't be afraid to give one.

If what the polls say are true, watching a movie and cuddling ranks at or near the top of the surveys. Does relationship building get any easier or any less expensive?

It's time to cuddle again! Start cuddling today and never stop!

"All you need is love."

~John Lennon

A Cuddle Bear Is Born

Three grown men were sitting in a room and rubbing their faces with various choices of teddy bear fur samples. It was weird and fun at the same time. Believe it or not, not all fur is soft. Our team finally found the cuddliest fur around, and our Cuddle Alert Bear was born.

After months of sketches and design work, the patience and labor were paying off big time. We were watching a cartoon-like bear take shape as a three-dimensional product. I had never been part of anything like this. It was exciting and creative. An idea that had rolled around in our heads was about to be fashioned into a cuddly bear for kids.

Thanks to the artistic work of Bob Simeone of Kidzink Studio and Mike Tucker of Media Connection, both in Dearborn, Michigan, we had a winning design and product.

We knew that we had a great idea for a bear, but now what?

With the help of WDIV-TV in Detroit and the Detroit Auto Dealers Association, we were able to launch an effort that was destined to help kids when and where they most needed it—a time of tragedy or trauma. Cuddle Alert Bears were placed in fire trucks and ambulances all across Southeast Michigan.

When a rescue worker pulled up to a trying scene and a kid was displaced or hurt, that rescue worker could take the edge off the situation by presenting the child with a bear. The idea worked, and over the course of the next two years, nearly eight thousand Cuddle Bears were given to fire departments for distribution.

Ingenuity met generosity, and children were helped and comforted.

I have heard it said that a man never stands so tall as when he gets down on a bended knee to help a child. That was so true in this case.

I want you to experience a Cuddle Bear yourself. Visit our website at www.cuddlealert.com to order various products, including books and Cuddle Bears.

There is no way to experience the cuddly fur on the bear without acquiring one for yourself or somebody you care about.

Chuck Gaidica is an Emmy Award–winning television and radio personality in Detroit, Michigan. He created the phrase "Cuddle Alert" as a fun call to action during cold-weather outbreaks. The alert is a platonic reason to cuddle with somebody for warmth and much more: a healthful connection of two souls. Chuck has spent years researching the connection between cuddling and our wellness. As a weather forecaster, Chuck has been issuing "Cuddle Alerts" on TV and radio for nearly thirty years. He has been seen on NBC's *Today Show* issuing a "Cuddle Alert" nationally. Chuck is America's cuddle expert and is a frequent motivational speaker.

Chuck and his wife, Susan, have five children and live in Northville, Michigan. They love their family and their dogs. They have a rich church life and a deep relationship with God. To find more information, visit www.cuddlealert.com.

A portion of the proceeds from this book, the Cuddle Alert program, and all of Chuck's projects will benefit charity.

Jeff Covieo has been drawing since he could hold a pencil and hasn't stopped since. He has a BFA in photography from the Center for Creative Studies in Michigan and works in the commercial photography field, though drawing and illustration have been his avocation for years. Other titles illustrated by Jeff include *Read to Me, Daddy! My First Football Book* and *The Ride of Your Life: Fighting Cancer with Attitude.*

Also by Chuck Gaidica,
Tommy Starts Something Big:
Giving Cuddles with Kindness.
www.cuddlealert.com